W9-DEZ-671

# GO WEST!
## Travel to the Wild Frontier

# GO WEST WITH COWBOYS AND RANCHERS

## Tim Cooke

# Crabtree Publishing Company
www.crabtreebooks.com

# Crabtree Publishing Company
## www.crabtreebooks.com

**Author:** Tim Cooke

**Consultant:** Professor Patricia Loughlin,
    University of Central Oklahoma

**Designer:** Lynne Lennon

**Picture Manager:** Sophie Mortimer

**Design Manager:** Keith Davis

**Editorial Director:** Lindsey Lowe

**Project Coordinator:** Kathy Middleton

**Editor:** Janine Deschenes

**Proofreaders:** Wendy Scavuzzo and Petrice Custance

**Children's Publisher:** Anne O'Daly

**Production coordinator and Prepress techician:** Tammy McGarr

**Print coordinator:** Katherine Bertie

Production coordinated by Brown Bear Books

**Photographs:**
Front Cover: **Alamy:** North Wind Picture Archives main;
**Getty Images:** Stanley Lange br; **Shutterstock:** tr.

Interior: **Corbis:** Bettmann 7tl; **Dreamstime:** Lee Robin 4bl, Debra Weeks 13; **Getty Images:** John C.H. Grabill 18; **Library of Congress:** 5, 6tl, 10, 15br, 17, 19t, 21tr, 21br, 25, 26tr, 27, 28, 29br; **Panoramio:** Leaflet 12; **Shutterstock:** Atomazul 23, M. Cornelius 7br, George Dukinas 6b, Joe Gough 19b, Stephen Rees 16tl, Lincoln Rogers 20, T Photography 29tl; **Thinkstock:** John Pitcher 15tr, M. Kucova 26br, Photos.com 11, Purestock 24br, P. Schoenfelder 14, Stockbyte 16cl, Marek Uliasz 4cr; **Topfoto:** The Granger Collection 16br, 22, 24tl.

All other artwork and maps **Brown Bear Books Ltd**.

Brown Bear Books has made every attempt to contact the copyright holder. If you have any information please contact licensing@brownbearbooks.co.uk

**Library and Archives Canada Cataloguing in Publication**

Cooke, Tim, 1961-, author
    Go West with cowboys and ranchers / Tim Cooke.

(Go West! travel to the wild frontier)
Includes index.
Issued in print and electronic formats.
ISBN 978-0-7787-2322-6 (bound).--
ISBN 978-0-7787-2335-6 (paperback).--
ISBN 978-1-4271-1732-8 (html)

    1. Cowboys--Juvenile literature.  2. Ranchers--Juvenile literature.  3. Cattle herders--Juvenile literature.  4. Frontier and pioneer life--Juvenile literature.  I. Title.

F596.C66 2016          j978          C2015-907966-7
                                     C2015-907967-5

**Library of Congress Cataloging-in-Publication Data**

Names: Cooke, Tim, 1961- author.
Title: Go West with cowboys and ranchers / Tim Cooke.
Description: New York : Crabtree Publishing, 2016. | Series: Go West! Travel to the wild frontier | Includes index. | Description based on print version record and CIP data provided by publisher; resource not viewed.
Identifiers: LCCN 2016001585 (print) | LCCN 2015049843 (ebook) | ISBN 9781427117328 (electronic HTML) | ISBN 9780778723226 (reinforced library binding : alk. paper) | ISBN 9780778723356 (pbk. : alk. paper)
Subjects: LCSH: Cowboys--West (U.S.)--History--19th century--Juvenile literature. | Longhorn cattle--West (U.S.)--History--19th century--Juvenile literature. | Cattle drives--West (U.S.)--History--19th century--Juvenile literature. | West (U.S.)--History--1860-1890--Juvenile literature. | Ranch life--West (U.S.)
Classification: LCC F596 (print) | LCC F596 .C746 2016 (ebook) | DDC 978/.02--dc23
LC record available at http://lccn.loc.gov/2016001585

## Crabtree Publishing Company
www.crabtreebooks.com          1-800-387-7650

Printed in Canada/022016/IH20151223

**Published in Canada**
**Crabtree Publishing**
616 Welland Ave.
St. Catharines, Ontario
L2M 5V6

**Published in the United States**
**Crabtree Publishing**
PMB 59051
350 Fifth Avenue, 59th Floor
New York, New York 10118

**Published in the United Kingdom**
**Crabtree Publishing**
Maritime House
Basin Road North, Hove
BN41 1WR

**Published in Australia**
**Crabtree Publishing**
3 Charles Street
Coburg North
VIC, 3058

# CONTENTS

# What Are the Prospects?

By the mid-19th century, the vast open spaces of the North American West seemed ideal for raising cattle to feed the growing populations.

## HOME ON THE RANGE

★ **Vast grasslands**

★ **Ideal for buffalo ... and cattle**

The "open range" was the name given to the grasslands of the Midwest. This extended from Wyoming and the Dakota Territory farther north into Canada, and down south into Texas. In the east, tall grass covered the **prairies**. In the west, treeless plains of short grass were broken by rocky areas, rivers, and canyons. The range was home to millions of buffalo—and ranchers discovered it was also ideal for raising cattle.

*Above: Cows could roam freely over the rich grasslands of the open range.*

## Cattle in Texas

★ **Small beginnings ...**

Spanish soldiers brought six cows to Mexico in 1521. By the time Texas declared independence from Mexico in 1836, there were six cows for every Texan. The herds on the open range kept growing. In 1866, railroads reached the West. Now, beef could be transported by railroad to sell in markets in the East. This made Texan cattle worth a lot more money.

# Barons of the West

★ **Ranchers seize the open range**

★ **Control huge areas**

After the American Civil War ended in 1865, ranchers began grazing their cattle on the range. Some bought patches of land that were spaced out. This helped them control large areas of the range. The ranchers were men such as John W. Iliff, who built the first open-range ranch in Wyoming in 1867. John Chisum opened the first ranch in New Mexico. Future president Theodore Roosevelt built a ranch in North Dakota. In Canada, Montreal **cattle baron** Matthew Cochrane led the push west to claim land for ranching in Alberta, Saskatchewan, and British Columbia.

*Above: By 1885, 35 cattle barons owned over 30,000 square miles (77,700 square kilometers) of the range.*

## COWBOYS WANTED!!

Men needed to look after cattle herds and drive them to the railroads.

★ Are you strong, self-motivated, and independent?

★ Are you a skilled horseman?

★ Are you willing to work hard for low pay (really, really low pay)?

**IF THE ANSWER IS YES, YOU COULD BE A COWBOY!**

## DID YOU KNOW?

Until 1836, Texas and the Southwest belonged to Mexico. The first cowboys were Mexican. Many words associated with cowboys come from Spanish words, including chaps, ranch, lasso, corral, and sombrero.

# Meet the Folks

Cowboys came from many backgrounds, but they all had to be tough. Most were also very young. On average, cowboys were just 24 years old.

## THE FIRST TRAIL

★ **Chisholm opens the way**

★ **Crosses Indian Territory**

The Cherokee trader Jesse Chisholm used Native American tracks to open a trail through Indian Territory, now Oklahoma. In 1867, Joseph G. McCoy opened **stockyards** on the railroad at Abilene, Kansas. Texas ranchers used Chisholm's 520-mile (837-km) trail to drive cattle to Abilene to be taken east by train. The demand for meat on the East Coast meant beef was worth ten times more out East than in Texas.

*Left: This 20th-century mural in Fort Worth, Texas, remembers the Chisholm Trail.*

## MY WESTERN JOURNAL

Imagine you are a rancher. Using evidence from this spread, write a job advertisement to recruit the ideal cowboy to work on your ranch.

# Tough Guys

★ **Bring a gun ...**

**... It might be useful**

Many cowboys were former soldiers from the Civil War. Others had been criminals. Ranchers preferred to hire cowboys who were good with guns so they could protect their herds from **rustlers** or wolves. No wonder some people thought cowboys were like outlaws.

# WHERE ARE YOU FROM?

★ **Wide mix of origins**

★ **Everyone welcome!**

Cowboys came from a range of backgrounds. Some were Mexican *vaqueros* who lived in what had only recently become US territory. They were joined by Native Americans, who were skilled horsemen used to hunting buffalo. About one-fifth of cowboys were African Americans, including former slaves from the South who wanted to start new lives in the West after the Civil War. Some cowboys came from Europe. They included the Mennonites. These Russian Christians were used to the harsh conditions of the **steppes**.

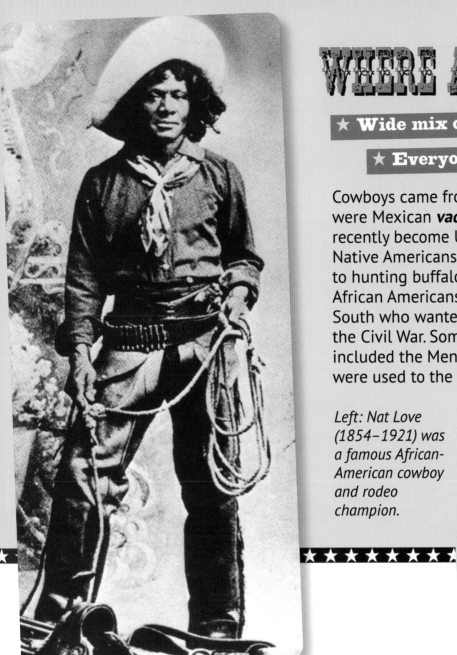

*Left: Nat Love (1854–1921) was a famous African-American cowboy and rodeo champion.*

## DID YOU KNOW?

Many cowboys found that life on the open range was too demanding. Only a third of all cowboys ever rode a trail twice. For the others, once was more than enough!

# Beware of Homesteaders!

★ **Farmers fence their land**

★ **Passage of cattle blocked**

As more people settled in the West, ranchers and cowboys clashed with new **homesteaders**. These farmers wanted to grow crops and raise animals. They used barbed wire to fence off their land from the range. The fences blocked cattle trails, often in key locations where herds could find water.

# Roads Most Traveled

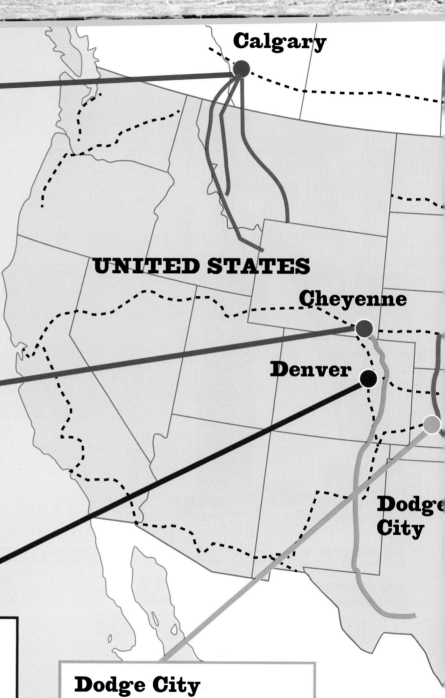

## Calgary
Between 1880 and 1885, cattle from Wyoming, Oregon, and Montana were driven north to stock Canadian ranches. After the Canadian Pacific Railway reached Calgary in 1883, cattle were taken by train to Toronto.

## Cheyenne
After the railroad reached Cheyenne in 1867, the town grew so quickly it became known as the "Magic City of the Plains." Cheyenne was the base of the Wyoming cattle ranchers who wanted to limit homesteader settlement of the range.

## Denver
Denver was settled in 1858 as a mining town. The railroad arrived in 1870, after citizens raised funds to build a 100-mile (160-km) link to the transcontinental railroad.

## Dodge City
Dodge City had a reputation for being a wild town. It was busiest in 1883 and 1884, when Kansas ruled that all cows had to be loaded onto railcars there.

UNITED STATES

Calgary

Cheyenne

Denver

Dodge City

For cowboys and ranchers, life was shaped by the trails that linked ranches to the railroads.

## Key

| | |
|---|---|
| ·············· | Major railroads |
| —— | Chisholm Trail |
| —— | Sedalia or Shawnee Trail |
| —— | Goodnight-Loving Trail |
| —— | Western Trail |
| —— | Trails to Calgary |

CANADA

Toronto

Chicago

Ellsworth

Abilene

## Chicago

Chicago was the heart of the cattle market. Millions of animals from the West were killed in its stockyards. The meat was packed in refrigerated railcars to keep it fresh, then shipped to towns and cities on the East Coast.

### Locator map

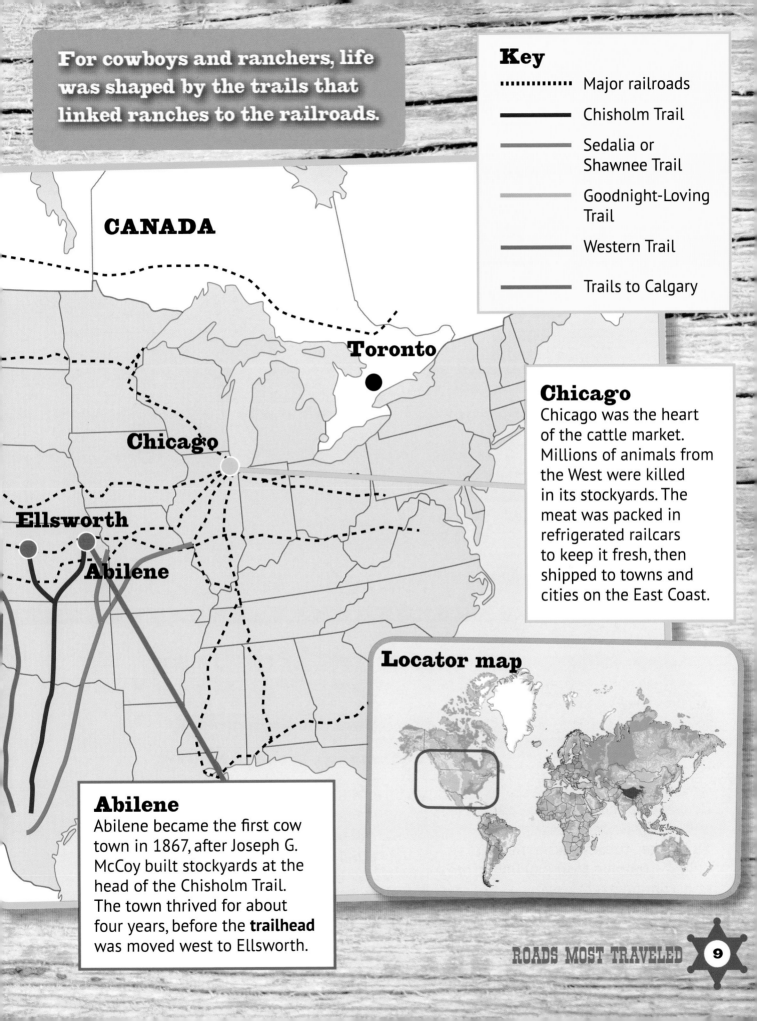

## Abilene

Abilene became the first cow town in 1867, after Joseph G. McCoy built stockyards at the head of the Chisholm Trail. The town thrived for about four years, before the **trailhead** was moved west to Ellsworth.

# Let's Get Going

As ranches were established in Texas, Montana, Wyoming, and elsewhere, a system of trails was created to move cattle to the railroads.

## Life on the Trail

★ **Crossing the country**

★ **Hard life for cowboys**

A herd on the trail usually had around 3,000 cattle and about 10 cowboys. The cattle covered about 12 to 15 miles (19–24 km) a day. The journey to the railroad could take up to four months. Cowboys might be in the saddle for 17 hours a day. At night, they stopped to feed and water the cattle. Cowboys ate beans and rice around a campfire before sleeping.

*Cowboys water cattle in a shallow river.*

## DID YOU KNOW?

Cattle on the trail could not be moved too quickly or they would lose weight. That meant they would be worth less when they were sold at the **railhead**.

## Me and My Horse

★ **More than one horse needed**

★ **Mustangs broken for drive**

A cattle drive was accompanied by a horse herd, known as a *remuda*. Each cowboy had eight to ten horses. He switched horses two or three times a day to rest them. Often the horses were wild **mustangs** that had to be trained before they could be ridden. The remuda was looked after by the **wrangler**, who was usually one of the youngest cowboys.

# DEADLY FEVER

★ **Tiny tick causes disease**

★ **Cattle kept out of states**

A **tick** that lived on Texas longhorn cattle caused a disease known as Texas Fever. The disease was fatal to cattle from the Midwest. In the 1850s, Kansas banned Texan cattle from entering the eastern part of the state, where most farms were located. In the mid-1880s, Kansas, Missouri, and Colorado all banned cattle from other states to protect their own cattle from the disease.

# TRAIL JOBS

★ **TRAIL BOSS:** Runs the whole cattle drive. Needs to be an expert navigator and good at discipline.

★ **POINT:** Two cowboys who ride at the head of the herd, leading the cattle.

★ **SWING OR FLANK:** Cowboys who ride at the sides of the herd, preventing cows from breaking away.

★ **DRAG:** Cowboys who follow the herd, making sure no cows are left behind. This is the dirtiest job, because of the dust. It is often done by the youngest cowboys.

★ **COOKIE:** The veteran cowboy in charge of cooking on the chuck wagon.

# END OF THE TRAIL

★ **Fun, fun, fun!**

★ **Cow towns welcome cowboys**

Whole towns were built where a trail reached the railroad. These cow towns were famous for being lawless. Some did not even have a sheriff. Dodge City in Kansas once had 24 gunfights in a single year. Cowboys whooped and hollered as they rode into town. Once they were paid, they usually got a bath, a haircut, and a beard trim or shave. Next stop was the outfitters for new clothes. Then it was off to celebrate. Cow towns such as Abilene, Kansas, had dozens of saloons.

*Abilene, at the end of the Chisholm Trail, was known as the wildest town in the West.*

# Out on the Open Range

The range extended from the Mississippi River to the Rocky Mountains. There were high plains in the north, and grasslands and rocky canyon lands in the south. Both landscapes provided good grazing for cattle.

## The High Plains

★ **Cattle replace buffalo**

★ **Montana and Wyoming attract ranchers**

Ranchers introduced cattle to the high plains of Montana and Wyoming in the 1880s. There was plenty of food, because white hunters had hunted the local wild buffalo close to **extinction**. The plains grass produced high quality beef. The arrival of the railroad in Cheyenne, Wyoming, allowed northern ranchers to sell their cows easily.

### DID YOU KNOW?

Many different kinds of grass grow in the West. The grasses are classified as tall, short, and mixed. Tall grasses grow as high as an adult human. Buffalo and cattle favored the short grasses of "buffalo country," farther west toward the Rockies.

## A TEXAS VALLEY

★ **Ideal short-grass grazing**

★ **The world's largest ranch**

Rancher Charles Goodnight found that the short grass in the Palo Duro Canyon in Texas was ideal for raising Texas longhorns. In 1876, he joined John Adair to set up the JA Ranch. By 1883, the JA was the largest ranch in the country. It covered over 1 million acres (404,686 ha) and had more than 100,000 cattle.

*Left: To make room for his cows, Charles Goodnight drove 10,000 buffalo from the Palo Duro Canyon in Texas.*

# Dangerous Rivers

Access to water was vital for cattle herds, but crossing a river was the most dangerous moment in any cattle drive. Herding cattle across Western rivers such as the Nueces, Guadalupe, Brazos, Wichita, and Red put cowboys and cattle at risk. Sometimes trails had shallow **fords**, where animals could walk across the river. At other times, cattle were loaded onto rafts and ferried across. This was slow and could be dangerous. Usually, cattle and horses had to swim across the river. They risked drowning or being swept away. Cowboys clung to their horses, since most cowboys were unable to swim.

*Above: Cows keep their heads above water as they swim across a river.*

# TAKE COVER!

★ **Wild weather in the West**

★ **Droughts, blizzards, tornadoes**

The plains suffered from extreme weather. They were battered by strong winds and **tornadoes**. Thunder and lightning could make cattle stampede. Winter brought blizzards, and cattle in the open could become stranded in deep snow drifts. A dry summer brought **drought**. Rivers dried up in the heat and cattle died from lack of water.

## MY WESTERN JOURNAL

Using the text on these pages, list the reasons why the plains were both suitable and unsuitable for raising cattle.

# Working with the Environment

Cowboys spent most of their working lives on the open range or on the trail. Even on the ranch, they were surrounded by the natural world.

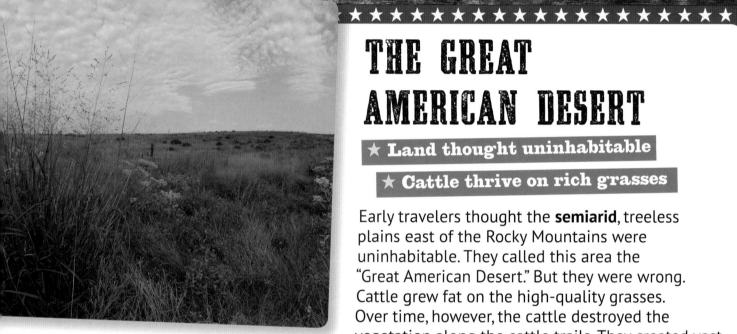

*Above: The grasslands had few water sources and little construction material to attract settlers.*

## THE GREAT AMERICAN DESERT

★ **Land thought uninhabitable**

★ **Cattle thrive on rich grasses**

Early travelers thought the **semiarid**, treeless plains east of the Rocky Mountains were uninhabitable. They called this area the "Great American Desert." But they were wrong. Cattle grew fat on the high-quality grasses. Over time, however, the cattle destroyed the vegetation along the cattle trails. They created vast dusty tracks that were hundreds of yards wide.

## Dress for the Elements

★ **Working in all weather**

Cowboys were outdoors in all weather conditions. They drove their herds in beating sun or driving snow and rain. They had to dress for protection. A wide-brimmed hat shielded them from the sun and the rain. Leather **chaps** and tall boots protected their legs from thorns and bushes as they rode.

### DID YOU KNOW?

Many cowboys thought a bandanna was their most valuable piece of clothing. It kept dust out of their mouth and the sun off their neck. It could be soaked in water for washing or drinking. It could even be made into a bandage or sling.

# NATURE'S DANGERS

★ **From the tiniest ticks ...**

**... to the largest wolves**

Cowboys had to protect their herds from many threats. There was little they could do about the tick that spread deadly Texas Fever. On the trail, they looked out for mountain lions and wolves that might attack the cattle. Gray wolves hunted in packs at dawn and dusk. Cowboys shot them on sight. If wild animals killed any cows, cowboys lost money from their pay.

# A Country Home

★ **Ranches built in isolated spots**

★ **Self-sufficiency essential**

Ranchers' homes could be hundreds of miles from any neighbors. A ranch had to provide the people and livestock living there with everything they needed. If possible, ranches were built near a creek. If not, ranchers dug deep wells and hauled water up in buckets or used windmills to pump water to the surface. There was often a vegetable patch. Most ranches had a timber barn to store feed for the animals, a **bunkhouse** for the cowboys, and workshops where equipment could be repaired. Horses were kept and trained in the **corral**.

*This small ranch has a windmill to pump water from a deep well.*

# Making Money

The rapidly growing North American population created a valuable market for western beef. Some people grew rich from the cattle trade— but they rarely included the cowboys.

## COWBOY ECONOMICS

★ **Money hard to earn ...**

**... but easy to spend**

Cowboys were paid when they arrived at the railhead. The money often did not last long after the hard months on the trail. Cowboys drank and gambled their money away in cow towns. Some spent everything they had earned in just a few days—then headed back to the ranch to start all over again.

# If You Build It, They Will Come

★ **Fortune-hunters develop the West**

★ **Cattle are the new gold**

As the railroads spread, businessmen saw a chance to make money. They included people such as Joseph G. McCoy, who ran stockyards. There were also people such as Lou and J. W. Gore, who ran the Drover's Cottage hotel in Abilene, Kansas. When Abilene lost its popularity as a cow town in 1871, they moved the hotel to nearby Ellsworth piece-by-piece on carts.

*Texas longhorns are loaded onto a railroad car in Abilene, Kansas, in 1871.*

# THE CENTER OF THE MEAT INDUSTRY

> ★ **Make tracks to Chicago**

> ★ **Nine railroads meet**

Most railroad lines from the West carried cattle to Chicago, from where meat was distributed throughout the East Coast. Nine railroad companies cooperated to build the Chicago Union Stockyards, which opened on Christmas Day in 1865. The site had 2,300 pens to keep the cattle, sheep, and hogs that arrived by railroad. By 1890, about nine million animals were butchered in the stockyards every year.

*Left: The stockyards in Chicago had thousands of pens. Cattle were transported there by rail from all over the West.*

# International Appeal

> ★ **Foreign investors join the rush**

> ★ **Newcomers do poorly**

In 1881, a cavalry officer named James Brisbin wrote *The Beef Bonanza, or How to Get Rich on the Plains*. The book persuaded many British readers to invest in Texas in the early 1880s. British companies bought up so much land in the state that part of Texas became known as "Little England." The newcomers were poor ranchers, however. They lost many cattle to rustlers. They were even tricked by their own cowboys, who told them they owned more cows than they actually did.

## DID YOU KNOW?

One valuable market for ranchers was selling beef to Native Americans. No longer able to hunt buffalo on the range, they had to buy their meat. When Native Americans were made to live on reservations, the government bought beef to feed them.

# Bed and Board

Cowboys did not earn much money, but their employers did provide them a place to sleep and something to eat. Their lives were not luxurious.

This small ranch was photographed in the Dakota Territory in the late 1880s.

## ON THE RANCH

★ **Welcome to our lovely home**

★ **Self-contained residence**

Cowboys usually lived on the ranch. The main house was home to the rancher and his family. Cowboys slept in a bunkhouse. This was a large open room full of narrow cots. There was coffee on the wood stove and often some postcards or photographs on the wall. The beds were often full of bedbugs and lice. When it was warm enough, some cowboys preferred to sleep outside.

## MY WESTERN JOURNAL

Look at the foods mentioned on these pages. Do you think you would have enjoyed eating like a cowboy? Give your reasons.

## Cookhouse comforts

★ **Fresh food ...** ... from underground

On larger ranches, the rancher's family and the cowboys ate in the same cookhouse. The food was prepared by the rancher's wife or by a hired cook. The cookhouse floor was stone, so it kept the room cool. This helped to preserve fresh food. Meat, vegetables, and fruit were sometimes kept in an underground cold room to keep them from spoiling.

# GRAB A BITE

★ **Home away from home**

★ **Good food on the go!**

When they were looking after cattle on the range in spring and fall, cowboys from different ranches worked together. They rode on their own all day. In the evening, they shared a meal at the chuck wagon. This was a wagon with an added "chuck box." The box had shelves for storage and a hinged lid that folded down to act as a table for food preparation. The chuck wagon carried a barrel of fresh water and wood for making cooking fires. The cook, or "cookie," was usually a veteran cowboy.

*Above: Cowboys in Colorado gather around the chuck wagon on the range.*

## MENU
### Try our cowboy favorites!

☞ **Beans**
☞ **Fresh Coffee**
☞ **Sourdough Biscuits**
☞ **More Beans**
☞ **Salt Pork**
☞ **Beef Jerky**
☞ **Even More Beans**
☞ **Tinned Peaches**

## DID YOU KNOW?

The chuck wagon is said to have been invented by the Texas rancher Charles Goodnight. He added a chuck box to a wagon when setting out on a cattle drive.

# Life as a Cowboy

Cowboys had their own forms of entertainment. Increasingly, however, they clashed with other people who were moving to the West.

Above: A cowboy holds tightly to the back of a bucking bronco during a modern rodeo.

## RODEO ROOTS

★ **Entertainment on the range ...**

**... becomes a modern sport!**

Most bosses banned drinking, gambling, and card games on the trail. To pass their spare time, cowboys competed to see who was quickest at **lassoing** a calf. They also held horse races. These contests led to the modern rodeo. The first organized rodeo was held in Cheyenne, Wyoming in 1897. It is still held today.

## DID YOU KNOW?

One or two cowboys kept watch over the herd at night. They sang softly as they rode among the cows. Slow ballads helped to keep the animals calm. Favorite songs included "Dinah Had a Wooden Leg" and "The Dying Cowboy." Cowboys also made up their own songs, using rude words.

## Straight Out of Texas

★ **All cowboys called Texans**

★ **Lone Star State dominated by ranchers**

So many cowboys came from Texas that "Texan" became another name for "cowboy". Texas had belonged to Mexico until 1836, when it declared independence. The **Texians** defeated the Mexican army and set up a republic. Even after they joined the Union in 1845, Texans were known for going their own way—just like most cowboys.

# Conflict on the Range

★ Ranchers vs settlers

★ Stockmen work together

In 1862, the Homestead Act gave settlers the right to 160 acres (65 ha) of free land in the West. As settlers claimed their land, they fenced it off. Ranchers objected to the fencing of the open range. They also tried to stop newcomers from grazing sheep on the range. They worked together to stop the settlers. In Texas, Charles Goodnight formed the Panhandle Stock Association. In Wyoming, wealthy ranchers formed the Cheyenne Club.

*Right: As settlers built homesteads on the range, ranchers worked together to try to stop them.*

# THAT'S ENTERTAINMENT!

★ **Traveling shows**

★ **The world's a stage!**

Cowboys loved any kind of entertainment. Cow towns were full of music. Shows with dancers were held in saloons and theaters. Some townspeople tried to bring "higher culture" to the cow towns by putting on plays. Amateur actors poured into cow towns such as Ellsworth, Kansas. Although most of the shows were terrible, some actors, such as Lola Montez, became stars. The showman Phineas T. Barnum also brought his traveling circus to towns. The circus included freak shows and exotic animals.

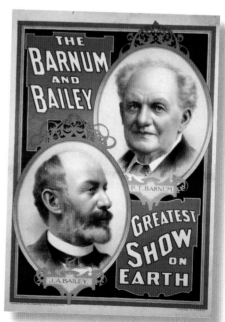

# Change and Conflict

The golden age of the cowboy lasted from the end of the Civil War in 1865 until the late 1880s. Those 20 years brought many changes to cowboy life.

## APPLYING SCIENCE

★ **Technology opens the plains**

★ **Inventions change the West**

A number of inventions changed the lives of cowboys and ranchers—for better or for worse.

★ **Railroads**
The transcontinental railroad was completed in May 1869. The railroads opened eastern markets for beef.

★ **Barbed Wire**
Joseph Glidden invented barbed wire in 1873. It made it easy for settlers to fence in their property on the open range.

★ **Refrigerated railcars**
Refrigerated railcars were perfected in 1878. Meat could then be kept fresh during longer journeys.

## The Great Die-Up

★ **Drought followed by blizzards**

★ **Thousands of cattle die**

After a drought in the summer of 1886, snow fell in Montana in November—and kept falling. About 5,000 starving cattle stormed into the town of Great Falls, searching for food. When the thaw came in March 1887, ranchers found that hundreds of thousands of cattle had frozen to death. The financial ruin of The Great Die-Up marked the end of open-range ranching.

*Ranches in Canada survived The Great Die-Up, only to face final ruin in the fierce winter of 1906.*

## DID YOU KNOW?

Cattle ranchers hired **range detectives**. These gunslingers were said to prevent rustling. In fact, they often picked on homesteaders, also called "nesters." The range detectives were rarely punished for their actions, even if they killed innocent homesteaders.

★ **Ranchers take a stand**

★ **War declared on settlers**

As settlers and ranchers clashed, violent conflicts broke out. They are often known as the **range wars**. In Johnson County, Wyoming, wealthy ranchers hired a group of gunmen known as "regulators" to attack settlers. Local homesteaders formed a **posse** of about 200 men to fight back. A number of homesteaders died. The violence lasted from 1889 until 1893. Eventually, the government sent the Sixth Cavalry to restore peace.

# GUNFIGHT AT THE O.K. CORRAL

★ **All over in 30 seconds...**

★ **Still famous today**

One of the most lawless cow towns was Tombstone, Arizona. It was the location of the most famous gunfight in history. The McLaury and Clanton brothers were local ranchers—and suspected cattle rustlers. They had a feud with Tombstone marshal Virgil Earp, his brothers Wyatt and Morgan, and their friend Doc Holliday. On the afternoon of October 26, 1881, the two sides met at the O.K. Corral. After 30 shots in 30 seconds, the two McLaury brothers and Billy Clanton were dead. Virgil and Morgan Earp were wounded.

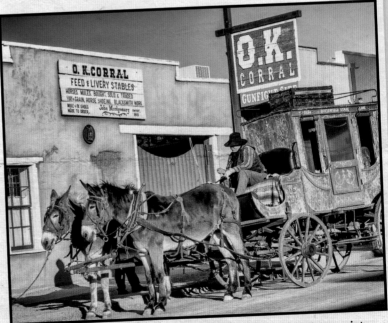

*The O.K. Corral has been preserved as a tourist attraction, thanks to the gunfight.*

# Dangerous Work

Daily life for cowboys was hard. In addition to tough conditions, predators, and extreme weather, they had to deal with stampedes and armed rustlers.

## STAMPEDE!

★ **Danger of death by crushing**

★ **Longhorns run wild**

The biggest threat on the trail was a **stampede**. A sudden noise could cause cows to run wildly. Cowboys galloped to the front of the herd to turn the cattle in a huge circle until they slowed down. It was dangerous work. Cowboys were often crushed and killed in stampedes.

*Left: In this illustration, a cowboy tries to control a stampede.*

## Dangers of the Range

★ **Perils on all sides**

★ **Look out for water**

Cowboys on the range faced many difficulties. Cows could become stuck in canyons or quicksand. It was easy to be injured while hauling them out. Rattlesnakes and predators also posed dangers. Drought was a serious threat, because many cattle and cowboys could die if water sources dried up. Cowboys looked for cottonwood trees (right). The trees were a sign that a water source was nearby.

### MY WESTERN JOURNAL

Imagine you are a cowboy on the range. Using information on these pages, write a letter home about the dangers you face at work.

*Cowboys use ropes to hold a calf down so that another cowboy can brand it.*

★ **Widespread rustling from herds**

★ **Brands "blotched" by thieves**

Before cattle were released onto the range, they were **branded**. A red-hot iron was used to burn the owner's mark into the animal's hide. These permanent marks meant cows from different ranches could graze together on the range and still be identified. However, rustlers soon started to "brand-blotch." They altered the original mark, and used the new brand to claim ownership of the cattle.

# Hired Guns

★ **Law and order, range style**

★ **Killers on the loose**

Ranchers in Texas and Wyoming worried about settlers invading their land. They blamed settlers for stealing cattle from their herds. The range detective Tom Horn was determined to stop anyone he thought might be a rustler. Horn got a reputation for shooting settlers dead. He killed as many as 17 men in Wyoming before he was finally hanged in 1903 for the murder of a teenage boy.

## DID YOU KNOW?

One threat to cowboy life came from state laws in Kansas. In the 1850s, Kansas established a line to mark how far east Texan cattle could be driven into the state. The line was meant to prevent Texas Fever from reaching the farms of western Kansas. In the 1880s, the line moved farther west. Eventually, Texan cattle were banned from Kansas.

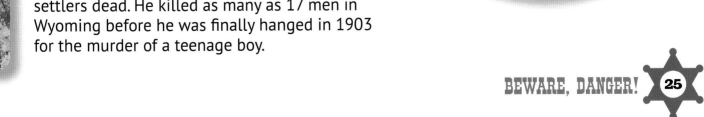

# Native Peoples

The creation of the cattle trails and the westward expansion of the United States severely affected the peoples who already lived on the plains.

## LIFE ON THE PLAINS

★ **Following the buffalo**

★ **Hunting with horses**

The plains were home to many Native peoples who lived by following the buffalo herds. Most Plains nations were **nomadic**. They used the buffalo for food, clothing, and shelter. Some Plains nations included Dakota, Lakota, and Nakota (Sioux), Kiowa, Comanche, and Cheyenne people and others. They were skilled horse riders. The coming of the cattle ranches disrupted this traditional way of life.

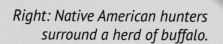

*Right: Native American hunters surround a herd of buffalo.*

## DID YOU KNOW?

Since the 16th century, Native American peoples worked as vaqueros for Spanish ranchers in Mexico. They were skilled horsemen who looked after herds of cattle.

# Living off the land

★ **Growing food ...**

**... settling communities**

Some Native peoples lived in more settled communities. Nations, including the Osage and Pawnee, grew crops such as corn and squash along valley bottoms. They also hunted buffalo and traded with neighboring peoples. Their lives were disrupted when settlers claimed their traditional lands.

# LOSING THEIR LANDS

## ★ Treaties made ...
## ... and broken

As settlers headed west, the US government created **treaties** that would ensure settlers could live on traditional Native American land. Some Native nations agreed to the treaties because they were given cash, or told their land would be safe. However, the government began to break these treaties. It took Native lands and forced Plains peoples to move to **reservations**. The Cheyenne were driven from their ancestral lands to Oklahoma. The Nez Percé were displaced to Kansas in 1877 after ranchers began to graze cattle in their homeland in the Pacific Northwest. As their buffalo food source disappeared from the prairies in Canada, First Nations had little choice but to sign treaties with the Canadian government and move to reserves.

*Above: When Nez Percé like this warrior were moved to a swampy part of Kansas, many died from fever and other disease.*

# War on the Plains

## ★ Resisting the invaders
## ★ Nations fight back

Some Native peoples fought the government's efforts to force them onto reservations. The Modoc of northern California fought the US Army from 1872–1873, but were defeated. Led by Sitting Bull, the Lakota also fought the army in 1876. The two sides clashed in what was called the Great Sioux War. On June 25, 1876, in what is now Montana, Native warriors killed General George Armstrong Custer and his cavalry in the Battle of the Little Bighorn. War ended when Sioux leader Kicking Bear surrendered in December 1890.

### MY WESTERN JOURNAL

Imagine you lived among the Plains peoples. Would you support signing a treaty with the US government, or would you oppose it? Give your reasons for or against.

# End of the Trail

As the West developed, ranchers and cowboys faced a rapidly changing way of life. The great age of ranching was over by the late 1880s—but the figure of the cowboy had become part of American history.

## End of the Range

★ **Plains overgrazed**

★ **Range fenced in**

By the middle of the 1880s, it was becoming more difficult for ranchers to graze cattle on the range. Settlers had fenced off parcels of land for homesteads, so the range had become smaller. There was less land for cattle to roam. On the range that was left, grass had often been overgrazed by cattle. Settlers had also introduced sheep to the range. They competed with the cattle for the best grass.

### DID YOU KNOW?

From the 1870s, farmers began to graze sheep on the range. The sheep farmers were often Mexican or Native American. Ranchers were worried that sheep would steal the best grass and spread disease. The ranchers attacked the newcomers in numerous clashes known as "sheep wars."

# Spreading Railroads

★ **Bringing stockyards to the West**

★ **No need for cattle trails**

Cattle drives finally ended in the late 1880s. They were no longer needed. The purpose of the original trails was to get cattle to the railroad. As the railroads spread, smaller lines and stockyards were built closer to where cattle were raised. This meant that the journey to get a herd to the railroad was far shorter and easier. Cowboys no longer rode the trail. They simply looked after the cattle on the ranch.

# THE RANGE TODAY

★ **Ranchers still ranching**

★ **Private and public land**

Cattle, sheep, and horse ranches still exist throughout the American West today. Ranchers own their own grazing lands or lease public or private rangelands for grazing cattle and sheep. They often use fences to subdivide their property for different uses, including pasture for the animals.

*Left: A cowboy herds Texas longhorns on a modern-day cattle ranch in the West.*

# THE GOLDEN WEST

★ **Myth of the cowboy**

★ **Symbol of independence**

Cowboys have become a symbol of American history. The first books about cowboys were written in the late 19th century. The books **romanticized** the figure of the cowboy. They were presented as strong, independent, resourceful, and honest. In the 20th century, western movies often showed cowboys in a similar way. In reality, cowboys were very poor and had a reputation for being criminals. In myth, however, the cowboys have become heroes of the American West.

*The cowboy has become a symbol of a tough, independent, and heroic character.*

# GLOSSARY

**branded** Given a permanent mark for identification

**bunkhouse** A building where workers sleep

**cattle baron** Powerful businessman who owns a large ranch

**chaps** Leather leggings that protect a horserider's legs

**corral** A fenced area for livestock

**drought** A long period without rainfall

**extinction** The dying-out of a species

**fords** Shallow places where people or animals can walk across rivers

**homesteaders** People who claim public land to build a home

**lassoing** Catching an animal with a rope

**mustangs** Small, light, wild horses

**nomadic** Describing people with no fixed home who instead move from place to place

**posse** A group of citizens who help a sheriff keep order

**prairies** Large, open areas of grassland

**railhead** A point where a road or water route reaches a railroad

**range detectives** Private security men hired by ranchers to protect their herds

**range wars** Armed conflicts between ranchers and homesteaders over the right to the range

**reservations** Areas of land set aside for Native Americans

**romanticized** Described in an idealized and appealing way

**rustlers** Thieves who steal cattle, horses, or other livestock

**semiarid** Having a limited amount of rainfall

**stampede** A sudden rush of panicking animals, particularly cattle

**steppes** Large, flat grasslands in eastern Europe or Siberia

**stockyards** Large yards with pens where livestock are kept before slaughter

**Texians** White settlers in the Republic of Texas

**tick** A small, insect-like parasite that lives on the body of a larger animal

**tornadoes** Strong winds that spin wildly in a funnel-shaped spiral

**trailhead** The place where a trail begins

**treaties** Agreements between governments

**vaqueros** The Spanish name for cowboys, usually applied to Mexicans

**wrangler** A cowboy in charge of horses

---

**May 20:** The Homestead Act offers free land in the West, encouraging settlement there.

**June:** For the first time, Texas ranchers drive cattle herds north to the railroads on the Goodnight-Loving and Shawnee trails.

**July:** Joseph G. McCoy opens stockyards at Abilene, Kansas, on the Kansas Pacific Railway. Abilene becomes the most popular destination for Texas ranchers using the Chisholm Trail.

**1862**    **1865**    **1866**    **1867**    **1868**    **1869**

At the end of the Civil War, huge herds of cattle roam the open range in Texas.

**November:** The Union Pacific Railroad reaches Cheyenne, Wyoming, encouraging ranching in the northern plains.

Kansas bans Texas cattle from the eastern part of the state to try to prevent the spread of Texas Fever.

## ON THE WEB

http://nationalcowboymuseum.
org/explore-category/the-cowboy/
A detailed overview of all aspects of
cowboy life, from the National Cowboy
& Western Heritage Museum in
Oklahoma.

http://texasalmanac.com/topics/
agriculture/cattle-drives-started-
earnest-after-civil-war
Gives the history of Texas cattle
drives from the Texas State Historical
Association.

http://www.history.com/topics/
cowboys
Introduction to cowboys and their
lives, with an index of links and
videos.

http://www.ducksters.com/history/
westward_expansion/cowboys.php
Describes the role cowboys played
in the westward expansion of the
United States.

## BOOKS

Kovacs, Vic. *A Cowboy's Life* (The True
History of the Wild West). PowerKids
Press, 2015.

Olson, Tod. *How to Get Rich on a Texas
Cattle Drive*. National Geographic
Children's Books, 2010.

Savage, Jeff. *American Cowboys*
(True Tales of the Wild West). Enslow
Publishers Inc., 2012.

Steele, Christy. *Cattle Ranching in the
American West* (America's Westward
Expansion). World Almanac Library, 2005.

In spring, large-scale buffalo hunting begins on the plains, opening more land for cattle.

Ellsworth replaces Abilene as the main cow town in Kansas.

A bitterly harsh winter in 1886–1887 causes the "Great Die-Up." Millions of cattle die, marking the end of open-range ranching.

**1870**    **1872**    **1874**    **1876**    **1886**

**February:** Abilene passes laws to control the wild behavior of cowboys who have just completed the Chisholm Trail.

**November 24:** Joseph Glidden is granted a patent for barbed wire, making it easier and cheaper for homesteaders to fence off the open range.

John Adair and Charles Goodnight open the JA Ranch in Palo Duro Canyon, Texas. It is the largest ranch in the country.

# INDEX